# Prayers of Love and Peace

**kevin mayhew**

May the angels and saints
who shine in radiant brightness
light up our path
and urge us on to heavenly virtues:

the virtues of peace and love,
devotion to you and justice to all,
wise friendship and a constant life,
faithful work and constant praise.

Love's furnace was hidden in a little room.
Homemaker God, come to our rooms this night.

Kindle in our hearts today
warmth of friendship, fire of love.
Burn away the dross, the fey.
Shine within, around, above.

Kindle in our work today
warmth of friendship, fire of love.
Burn away the dross, the fey.
Shine within, around, above.

Kindle in our world today
warmth of friendship, fire of love.
Burn away the dross, the fey.
Shine within, around, above.

Babe of heaven, defenceless Love,
you had to travel far from your home –
strengthen us on our pilgrimage of trust on earth.
King of glory, you accepted such humbling,
clothe us with the garments of humility.
Your birth shows us the simplicity of the Father's love,
keep us in the simplicity of that love.
Your coming shows us the wonder of being human,
help us to cherish every human life.

Thrice holy God, eternal Three in One,
make your people holy, make your people one.
Stir up in us the flame that burns out pride and power,
restore in us the trust that brings the servant heart
to flower.
Thrice holy God, come as the morning dew,
inflame in us your love
that draws all lesser loves to you.

Holy, holy, holy is the eternal flame undying,
burning here among us in sacrificial love.

Kindle in our hearts, O God,
the flame of that love which never ceases,
that it may burn in us
until we shine for ever in your presence.

*After a prayer of Columbanus.*

Dearest Christ,
the earth gave you a cave,
the skies gave you a star,
the angels gave you a song,
and we give you our love.

*Echoes an Orthodox liturgy.*

Flame of seeing,
light us up.
Flame of wisdom,
light us up.
Flame of peace,
light us up.
Flame of love,
light us up.

I am giving you love with my whole desire.
I am giving you affection with all my senses.
I am giving you honour with my whole heart.
I am giving you assent with my whole mind.
I am giving you my soul, O God of all gods.

My thought, my deed,
my word, my will,
my understanding, my intellect,
my way, my state.

*Echoes a prayer in The Carmina Gadelica.*

Christ of the scars of love,
into your hands
we place those who have been scarred by life:
those who have been betrayed,
those who have suffered loss of limb or esteem.

Christ of the scars of love,
into your hands
we place unwanted babies,
neighbours defamed, lovers spurned.

Christ of the scars of love,
into your hands
we place those who are victims of violence,
sharp practice or false accusation.

Holy Spirit, renew in us
joy in our work
life in our being
love in our relationships.

I bring my money to you, God, as a gift from heaven.
The Giver be on you, gift of heaven.
The Redeemer be on you, gift of heaven.
The Counsellor be on you, gift of heaven.
Thought be on you, gift of heaven.
Restraint be on you, gift of heaven.
Wisdom be on you, gift of heaven.

Loving Saviour, show yourself to us,
that, knowing you,
we may love you as warmly in return,
may love you alone, desire you alone,
contemplate you alone by day and night,
and keep you always in our thoughts.
May affection for you pervade our hearts.
May attachment to you take possession of us all.
May love of you fill all our senses.
May we know no other love except you who are eternal.
A love so great that the many waters of land and sea
will fail to quench it.

*Columbanus*

Lord Jesus Christ, truly human, truly God,
you unite in yourself humanity and God.
You prayed for the unity of all who believe.
May your churches, rejoicing in the unity of heaven,
attain communion around one table
and unite the world in a fellowship of peoples.

Through your Church, nurture us.
Through her pastors, nourish us.
Through her teachers, establish us.
Through her prophets, envision us.
Through her saints, sanctify us.

God help us to:
listen to our loved ones,
play with our loved ones,
laugh with our loved ones,
weep with our loved ones,
forgive our loved ones,
perform our duties to our loved ones,
be faithful to our loved ones,
and to increase the circle of our loved ones.

God of the earth
forgive us for becoming proud and disconnected
from your seed-bed of wisdom, nurture and life.

Help us always to know and feel that we are of the earth.
May we live this day as your humus.

Dearest Christ, you have given love,
given it exquisitely.
In your tiredness you washed your friends' tired feet.
In your generosity you gave bread to your betrayer.
In your all-seeing provision
you bequeathed a sacrament of bread and wine
that makes you constantly present to us.
In your anguish in the garden you fought with demons
and shared your doubt.
In your prayers you ever place your people in the
Divine Heart.
You call us to watch and pray.
Out of love for you we will watch and pray,
we will watch and pray.

Teach me when to be silent and when to speak.

When to listen and when to leave,

when to praise and when to refrain,

when to laugh and when to weigh,

when to tell and when to wait.

Give me the ambition

to use everything I have for the highest purposes,

to abuse no person,

to misuse no powers,

to harness skills to service,

and to bring great things to flower.

Risen Christ, I welcome you.
You are the flowering bough of creation;
from you cascades music like a million stars,
truth to cleanse a myriad souls.
From you flee demons, omens and all ill will;
around you rejoice the angels of light.

I rise up clothed in strength of Christ.
I shall not be imprisoned, I shall not be harmed,
I shall not be down-trodden, I shall not be left alone,
I shall not be tainted, I shall not be overwhelmed,
I go clothed in Christ's white garments.
I go freed to weave Christ's patterns.
I go loved to serve Christ's weak ones.

Spirit of God,

the breath of creation is yours.

Spirit of God,

the groans of the world are yours.

Spirit of God,

the wonder of communion is yours.

Spirit of God,

the fire of love is yours.

And we are filled.

Power of all powers, we worship you.
Light of all lights, we worship you.
Life of all lives, we worship you.

Maker of all creatures, we honour you.
Friend of all creatures, we honour you.
Force of all creatures, we honour you.

Love before time, we adore you.
Love in dark times, we adore you.
Love in present time, we adore you.

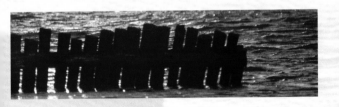

Deep harmony of the forest be mine.
Childlike love for God's creatures be mine.
Growing trust in God's providence be mine.

Bountiful Provider,

take penny-pinching from me.

Give me a generous heart and a helping hand

for every person and every creature I meet.

And thank you that this will bring blessing.

Merciful Father,

pour out your compassion through us,

that we may be instruments to set others free:

those who walk through life

with their feet in fetters,

clobbered with unjust burdens,

captives in prisons of body or spirit.

18

Three of forgiving love,
we lay the fragments of our lives at your feet.

In each hidden thought our minds start to weave,
be our canvas and our weaver.

In each wounded memory to which we cleave,
be our counsel and our healer.

Holy God, holy and mighty,
you can bring a holy child to birth in a barren womb.
You can bring a new thing to birth in a barren land.
Bring to birth in me that new thing that is your will.

Infinite One of the wise heart,
Saving One of the clear sight,
Knowing One of the hidden deeps:
may I learn from you as an eager pupil;
may I learn from life as a humble child;
may I learn from wise ones as a trusting friend;
may I learn from stillness as a silent listener.

Christ, victim of barriers,
Christ, vanquisher of barriers,
Christ, linking us across the shores,
of treachery and time –
make in us your home.

Child of Humanity,
Trinity's only Son,
gentle and strong,
from whose line we were born,
bring your peace to your warring children.

Peace between believers.
Peace between neighbours.
Peace between lovers.
In the love of the King of Life.

Peace between victor and vanquished.
Peace between wives and husbands.
Peace between parents and children.
The peace of Christ above all peace.

Toughen me, Lord.
Give me a heart of love
but a backbone of steel.

Holy God, holy and mighty,
strip from me all that is false and out of place.
Strengthen my roots in you,
bring me to that place
where I desire you alone.

Lord Spirit,

show me the things that are crooked in my life.

Lord Judge,

spare me from things that could be crooked in my life.

Lord Christ,

straighten out the things that are crooked in my life.

Three of Love,

keep me this day in your straight paths.

God of heroic love,

kindle in us the adventure of obedience,

the single eye,

the humble and generous heart,

which marked your saints.

Great Spirit, water the world.

Revive our dryness.

Soak our soreness.

Refresh our tiredness.

Wash our uncleanness.

Bathe our woundedness.

Immerse us in your love.

In the strength of the Warrior God
may I oppose all that pollutes.

In the eye of the Face of God
may I expose all that deceives.

In the love of the Servant God
may I bind up all that is broken.

God of gods,

establish your presence among us.

God of gods,

may your fire purge the wastelands.


God of gods,

may your people advance from one virtue to another.

God of gods,

may the kingdoms of this world become

the kingdom of our God.


God of gods,

helps us to grow today in patience and prayerfulness.

God of gods,

help us to grow today in wisdom and understanding.

Compassionate God of eternity,
free this place from bad influences of the past.

Compassionate God of heaven's powers,
screen us from people who wish us harm.

Compassionate God of freedom,
free us from curses and false predictions.

God of time, God of the saints,
you alone are stronger than the elements,
stronger than the shadows,
stronger than the fears.

Jesus of Love,

born of Mary,

proclaimed by apostles,

witnessed to by martyrs,

we bless you for your birth

and for your continuing presence with us.

In union with the many witnesses who give

their life for you,

may we make with them the seamless journey

from the Cradle to the Cross to the Crown.


Peace-making God,

may we, like your saints,

become peacemakers and hospitality givers,

open to change and partnership,

Spirit-led in solitude and costly service.

Enter deeply into our lives

until they reflect your peace on earth.

Thank you for the holy family –
Mary, Joseph, Jesus and the others.
May families reflect their dedication to put your will first.
May purity, trust and love grow strong in our households.

Thank you for the prophetess Anna
who, honed in daily attunement to you
in the offering of prayer and praise,
discerned your presence in an ordinary
but significant moment.
Take our senses, hone our intuition,
steep us in the disciplines of the Spirit,
that we may see your hand at work
in the events of today and tomorrow.

Thank you for the sanctuaries Egypt
offered to the holy family,
for their acquaintances with God-honourers
of another land and religion,
for the hermits and holy people of the deserts.
We pray for God honourers
who seek to welcome your servants in Egypt
and in Muslim lands;
for refugees; for hermits and others
who pattern an alternative way to our acquisitive society.

Thank you for the home in Nazareth,
and for the boy Jesus growing in skills of carpentry
and in the confidence of puberty.
We pray for young people
who are confused, de-skilled, orphaned,
and who know neither themselves or their calling;
may they find affirming adults to be alongside them.

Thank you that even at the death of Jesus
the holy family grew
through the adoption of John into Mary's family.
We pray for those who have died,
and for those who face loss of life or limb or hope.
May the healing light of Christ shine upon them,
and may they come to know that there is a family
more wonderful
than any they have known.

Take my hands, dear Christ,
that your compassion may flow through them out to others.

With these hands give tender touch
to those who are forgotten.
With these hands give warmth
to those left out in the cold.
With these hands shield your messengers
from ills that would attack them.
With these hands dispel darkness from the old.

Take my hands, dear Christ,
that your compassion may flow through them out to others.
With these hands please heal a lost and hurting world.

The God of peace go with us
to protect us from ill,
to keep our hearts still,
to strengthen our will.

May the Christ who walks with wounded feet,
walk with us on the road.
May the Christ who serves with wounded hands
stretch out our hands to serve.
May the Christ who loves with the wounded heart
open our hearts to love.

*Anon*

First published in 2005 by

KEVIN MAYHEW LTD
Buxhall, Stowmarket, Suffolk, IP14 3BW
E-mail: info@kevinmayhewltd.com
Website: www.kevinmayhew.com

9 8 7 6 5 4 3 2 1 0

ISBN 1 84417 419 0
Catalogue No. 1500810
Designed by Chris Coe
Edited by Marian Reid

Printed and bound in China

Ray Simpson is a co-founder of the worldwide
Community of Aidan and Hilda and is its first guardian.
He lives on Lindisfarne, where the Community has a
retreat and guesthouse: The Open Gate, Holy Island,
Berwick-upon-Tweed, TD15 2SD.
The Community's website is www.aidan.org.uk